FUN FACT FILE: SPACE!

20 FUN FACTS ABOUT GAS GIANTS

By Arielle Chiger and Matthew Elkin

Gareth Stevens
PUBLISHING

Please visit our website, www.garethstevens.com. For a free color catalog of all our high-quality books, call toll free 1-800-542-2595 or fax 1-877-542-2596.

Library of Congress Cataloging-in-Publication Data

Chiger, Arielle.
20 fun facts about gas giants / by Arielle Chiger and Matthew Elkin.
p. cm. — (Fun fact file: space!)
Includes index.
ISBN 978-1-4824-1002-0 (pbk.)
ISBN 978-1-4824-1003-7 (6-pack)
ISBN 978-1-4824-1001-3 (library binding)
1. Outer planets — Juvenile literature. 2. Jupiter (Planet) — Juvenile literature. 3. Saturn (Planet) — Juvenile literature. I. Chiger, Arielle. II. Title.
QB681.C45 2015
523.4—d23

First Edition

Published in 2015 by
Gareth Stevens Publishing
111 East 14th Street, Suite 349
New York, NY 10003

Copyright © 2015 Gareth Stevens Publishing

Designer: Sarah Liddell
Editor: Greg Roza

Photo credits: Cover, p. 1 Chris Walsh/The Image Bank/Getty Images; p. 5 Aaron Rutten/Shutterstock.com; pp. 6, 7 (stars) Procy/Shutterstock.com; pp. 6, 7, 12, 14, 21, 26 (Uranus and Jupiter), 27 (Saturn and Neptune) Tristan3D/Shutterstock.com; pp. 8, 15 CVADRAT/Shutterstock.com; p. 9 Orla/Shutterstock.com; p. 10 bluecrayola/Shutterstock.com; p. 11 (Neptune) MarcelClemens/Shutterstock.com; p. 11 (figure skater) Photodisc/Photodisc/Thinkstock.com; p. 13 narvikk/E+/Getty Images; p. 16 (main) Universal History Archive/ Universal Images Group/Getty Images; p. 16 (Ganymede) Universal History Archive/Contributor/Universal Images Group/Getty Images; p. 17 Ian McKinnell/Photographer's Choice RF/Getty Images; p. 18 Jamie Cooper/Contributor/SSPL/Getty Images; p. 19 Stocktrek/Stockbyte/Getty Images; p. 20 photo courtesy of NASA/JPL-Caltech/Space Science Institute; p. 22 BlueRingMedia/Shutterstock.com; p. 23 Diego Barucco/ Shutterstock.com; p. 24 Time Life Pictures/Contibutor/The LIFE Picture Collection/Getty Images; p. 25 Guido Amrein, Switzerland/Shutterstock.com; pp. 26–27 (stars) Mihai-Bogdan Lazar/Shutterstock.com; p. 29 SCIENCE SOURCE/Photo Researchers/Getty Images.

Printed in the United States of America

CPSIA compliance information: Batch #CS15GS: For further information contact Gareth Stevens, New York, New York at 1-800-542-2595.

Contents

Words in the glossary appear in **bold** type the first time they are used in the text.

Solid Earth

Earth is a **terrestrial** planet, which means it's made up mostly of rocks, soil, and metals and has a hard surface. Mercury, Venus, and Mars are terrestrial planets, too. The rocky planets, as we commonly call them, are the four planets closest to the sun.

The planets farther away from the sun than Mars are different. They're gas giants! Jupiter, Saturn, Uranus, and Neptune have far less solid **material** than the rocky planets. We would never be able to live on them—or even land on them!

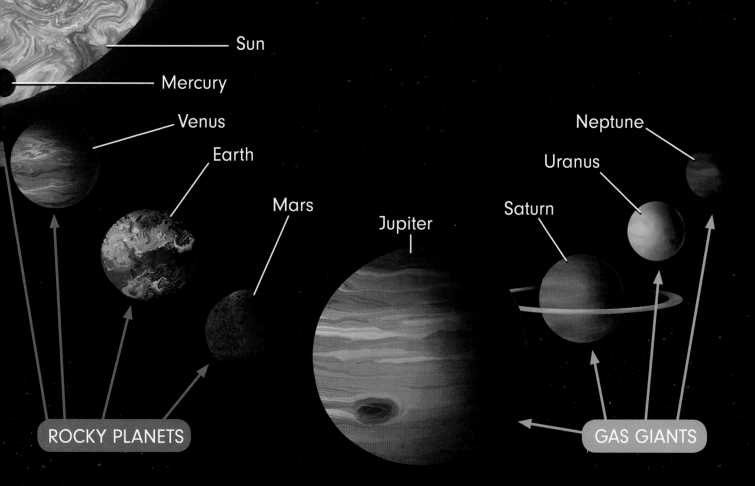

Together, the rocky planets, gas giants, and other space objects orbit, or circle, the sun. This is our solar system.

Sun

Mercury

Venus

Earth

Mars

Jupiter

Saturn

Uranus

Neptune

ROCKY PLANETS

GAS GIANTS

FACT 1

The gas giants in our solar system are named after giant Greek and Roman gods.

The gas giants are called Jovian planets. The ancient Roman god Jove (or Jupiter) was king of the gods. Saturn was a Roman god of farming. Uranus was the Greek god of the sky. Neptune was the Roman god of the sea.

Jupiter

Saturn

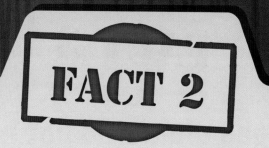
The gas giants would not make a good home for people.

Jupiter, Saturn, Uranus, and Neptune are made mostly of gases. They contain a lot of hydrogen and helium, which are the two most common kinds of matter in the **universe**. Planets made mostly of these gases can't possibly support life as we know it.

Uranus

Neptune

Hydrogen and helium can also be found on Earth, but in much smaller amounts.

The gas giants do not have a hard surface like the terrestrial planets.

If you could parachute through the **atmosphere** of a gas giant, you wouldn't land on the surface. You'd pass through it and keep falling! The matter in a gas giant gets more **dense** the closer you are to the **core**.

The closer to the gas giant's core, the more matter there is. It gets pressed more tightly together the deeper you go. Deep down, the gas giants likely have solid cores.

The sun contains over 99 percent of the matter in our solar system. Jupiter, the solar system's biggest planet, has about 1/1,000 the mass of the sun.

The gas giants were formed by matter leftover from when the sun formed.

When the solar system first formed over 4.5 billion years ago, energy from the sun began to push dust and gases out into space. Much of the leftover solid matter formed the closer, rocky planets. Much of the gases clouded together to form the gas giants.

FACT 5

Days on the gas giants are shorter than days on Earth.

The gas giants **rotate** faster than the rocky planets. It takes Jupiter about 10 hours to make one

complete rotation. This makes

1 day on Jupiter shorter

than an Earth day,

which is about

24 hours long.

A day on Saturn lasts about 11 hours. A day on Uranus lasts about 17 hours. A day on Neptune lasts about 16 hours.

When this figure skater pulls her arms in, she spins faster. This helps explain why the gas giants spin so quickly.

FACT 6

The gas giants have something in common with figure skaters.

The gas giants might be bigger than the rocky planets, but their matter is less dense. **Astronomers** believe each planet's core is small and dense. This makes the gas giants spin faster than the rocky planets. This is kind of like when a skater pulls in his or her arms to spin faster.

FACT 7

Gas giants are a bit flatter than rocky planets.

The gas giants spin so fast that their matter bulges out at the **equator**, where the speed is greatest. The poles flatten out. Because of this, the gas giants, especially Jupiter and Saturn, are more oval shaped than the rocky planets.

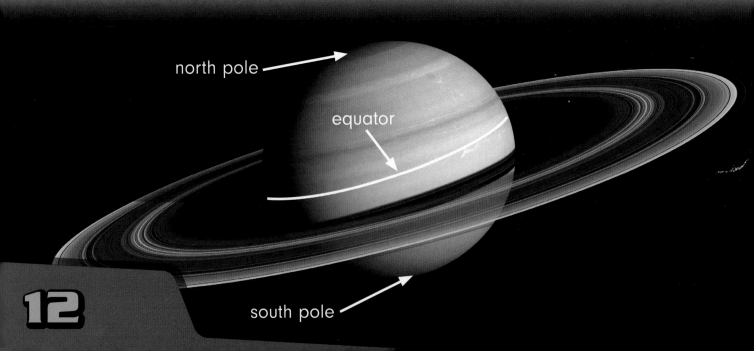

north pole

equator

south pole

Neptune was discovered in 1846. In July 2011, it finally completed the first full orbit since it was discovered.

gas giant	time it takes to orbit the sun once
Jupiter	11.8 Earth years (1 year on Jupiter)
Saturn	29.5 Earth years (1 year on Saturn)
Uranus	84 Earth years (1 year on Uranus)
Neptune	164.9 Earth years (1 year on Neptune)

FACT 8

A single year on a gas giant is much longer than a year on Earth.

Jupiter is more than five times farther away from the sun than Earth. Neptune, the most distant planet in the solar system, is about 30 times farther away! Gas giants have to travel much farther to complete a single orbit. This makes 1 year on them very long.

Biggest of Them All

FACT 9

About 1,320 Earths could fit inside Jupiter.

Jupiter is the closest gas giant to Earth. It's also the largest planet in the solar system. Jupiter has 2.5 times more mass than the rest of the planets combined. It would take 11.2 Earths lined up side by side to equal Jupiter's **diameter**.

Earth

Jupiter

This picture gives you an idea of how big Jupiter really is.

Great Red Spot

FACT 10

Jupiter's Great Red Spot is the largest and longest-lasting storm in the solar system.

Jupiter's atmosphere is very active. Jupiter has hot spots and cold belts, which create bands of color on its surface. Huge storms swirl close to its equator. The Great Red Spot is a gigantic hurricane! It has been there for more than 400 years.

Ganymede

One of Jupiter's moons, Ganymede, is the largest moon in the solar system. It's even bigger than the rocky planet Mercury.

FACT 11

Jupiter has many "children."

Jupiter's **gravity** is very strong. It pulls other space objects toward it. Some of these objects now orbit Jupiter. We call them moons. As of 2014, scientists had discovered 67 moons around Jupiter! There might be even more.

FACT 12

If you could drop it in a bathtub of water, Saturn would float.

Saturn is the second-largest planet in the solar system. However, it's also the least dense planet. Its matter isn't packed very tightly. Saturn is less dense than water. That means it could float in water...if there were an ocean big enough to hold it!

The chemicals that make up Saturn's atmosphere consist mostly of ammonia and ice. This gives it a yellowish appearance.

FACT 13

You can see Saturn's rings with a telescope.

After Earth, Saturn might be the best-known planet in our solar system because of its beautiful rings. Even though the other three gas giants also have rings, none are as brilliantly colored or as easy to see as Saturn's. You can even see them with a simple telescope.

This photograph of Saturn and a few of its moons was taken in 2006 using a 14-inch telescope and a webcam.

FACT 14

Saturn's rings are not solid.

Saturn's rings look solid from Earth. However, they're made up of bits of ice, rocks, and dust that range in size from incredibly tiny to as large as a big house. As the bits orbit Saturn, they bump together and break up larger pieces.

This photograph was taken by an unmanned spacecraft in 2013.

FACT 15

The north pole of Saturn is surrounded by a giant hexagon.

Just like Jupiter, the surface of Saturn is a stormy place. The gas giant's north pole is surrounded by a six-sided shape, or hexagon. Scientists have discovered that this shape is caused by wind currents on Saturn.

Uranus and Neptune are so cold they are sometimes called ice giants.

Uranus and Neptune are very far from the sun, and they're very cold. The atmosphere of both planets contains a gas called methane, which makes them look blue. These planets are so cold that their gases form ices and thick liquids beneath their surface.

Uranus

Neptune

Uranus and Neptune are so similar that they're often called sister planets.

21

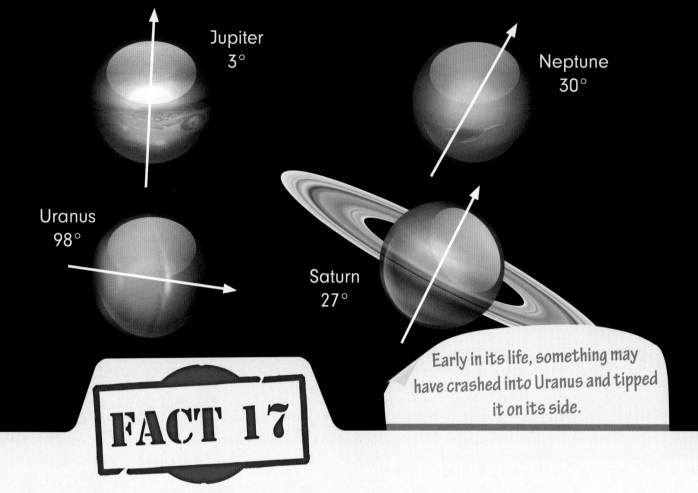

Jupiter
3°

Neptune
30°

Uranus
98°

Saturn
27°

Early in its life, something may have crashed into Uranus and tipped it on its side.

FACT 17

Long ago, Uranus tripped and fell over.

Uranus is different from the other planets in that its **axis** is tipped to the side. This means its poles rather than its equator face the sun. Orbiting the sun like this, one pole gets about 42 years of sunlight, followed by 42 years of darkness.

Neptune is so far away it can't be seen without a telescope.

Most of the planets were known to ancient astronomers because they were visible in the night sky. Even Uranus can be seen when things are just right. Scientists **predicted** that Neptune existed before they even saw it because of the way it affects Uranus's orbit.

Uranus speeds up when it gets nearer to Neptune and slows down when it moves away from Neptune. That's why scientists knew something else was out there.

Neptune has a very active atmosphere.

While Uranus looks mostly blue to us, Neptune has some interesting surface features. Fast-moving bands of white clouds in the atmosphere cast shadows on the planet's surface. Neptune has giant storms similar to Jupiter. They look like dark spots on the surface.

Great Dark Spot

clouds

Astronomers call Neptune's largest storm the Great Dark Spot.

FACT 20

Some astronomers think our solar system once had five gas giants.

Computer **simulations** of our solar system show that it may have had a larger gas giant at one time. Simulations show that the planets were much closer together. A brush with Jupiter kicked the fifth gas giant out of the solar system and helped the other planets move to their current locations.

Astronomers who think the fifth gas giant existed say it helped bring order to the solar system. Without it, Earth might have crashed into Mars or Venus long ago.

What Do You Know About the Gas Giants?

Astronomers have discovered many fun facts about the gas giants.

URANUS
- known as an ice giant
- looks blue due to methane in its atmosphere
- rings weren't discovered until 1977
- tipped on its side

JUPITER
- largest planet in the solar system
- Great Red Spot is largest storm in the solar system
- has most moons of any planet in the solar system
- bands of color

SATURN

- second-largest planet in the solar system
- has six main rings, made up of thousands of smaller rings
- density is lower than water
- hexagon shape at north pole

NEPTUNE

- known as an ice giant
- looks blue due to methane in its atmosphere
- takes almost 165 years to orbit the sun
- storms and clouds visible on its surface

27

Bon Voyage!

The gas giants are hard to study because they're so far away. Only one unmanned spacecraft has visited all the gas giants. Launched in 1977, *Voyager 2* is now approaching the outer limits of the solar system. This craft passed each of the gas giants and made exciting new discoveries about them.

Astronomers have learned a lot about our solar system by studying the gas giants. As telescopes improve in the years to come, they hope to learn even more.

This drawing shows *Voyager 2* as it approaches Neptune and its moon, Triton.

29

Glossary

astronomer: a person who studies stars, planets, and other heavenly bodies

atmosphere: the mixture of gases that surrounds a planet

axis: an imaginary straight line around which a planet turns

core: the central part of something

dense: packed very closely together

diameter: the distance from one side of a round object to another through its center

equator: an imaginary line around a planet that is the same distance from the north and south poles

gravity: the force that pulls objects toward the center of a planet or star

material: the kinds of matter something is made up of

predict: to guess what will happen in the future based on facts or knowledge

rotate: to turn around a fixed point

simulation: reproducing the features or actions of something, as with a computer

terrestrial: having to do with solid land

universe: everything that exists

For More Information

Books

Aguilar, David A. *Space Encyclopedia: A Tour of Our Solar System and Beyond.* Washington, DC: National Geographic, 2013.

Dartnell, Lewis. *My Tourist Guide to the Solar System and Beyond.* New York, NY: DK Publishing, 2012.

Websites

Our Universe
www.esa.int/esaKIDSen/OurUniverse.html
Learn more about our universe from this interactive website.

Planets for Kids
www.planetsforkids.org
Find lots more information about all the planets on this website.

Index